T0149379

RESONANCE OF THE
SOULS

Mahrukh Laeeq (Mahrukh Mustansar)

authorHOUSE®

AuthorHouse™
1663 Liberty Drive
Bloomington, IN 47403
www.authorhouse.com
Phone: 1 (800) 839-8640

Published by AuthorHouse 12/03/2018

ISBN: 978-1-5462-6904-5 (sc)
ISBN: 978-1-5462-6966-3 (e)

Library of Congress Control Number: 2018913695

Print information available on the last page.

Contents

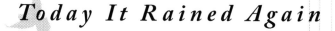

Today It Rained Again

When it rains, it leaves the fragrance of few words
that bond which is no more,
a girl leaning on someone,
betraying herself for one person,
leaves that bleak season where someone is a survival reason
and a promise that is treason, a life that shows grief is a treasure;

where an everlasting hope can't be measured
leaving the sky blue, where happiness is hard to choose,
it falls down her tears, secures her insecure fears,
and tells, *"how she got insane."*

Listen! TODAY IT RAINED AGAIN!

Mahrukh Laeeq

Smoke Screens

If you miss him
for the relationship skid,
only your eyes would blur
on the faults he did.

If you miss him
for the words unheard,
then you would miss him
for every look, he slurred.

If you miss him
for his decoyed mind,
then you would miss him
for making you blind.

But if you miss him
for his smoky love,
then you would grief
for the feelings, all above.

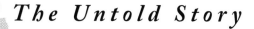

The Untold Story

I saw a girl smiling all the time,
her actions were very sweet but very naïve.
Promising and funny was her attitude,
but, I saw her weeping in the solitude.

The day she dreamt that day she wept,
there was something going around.

A hopelessness was all that surrounds,
she was strong but someone was her weakness,
She was on thorns but everyone was heedless.

he was the one, who was her pain,
her emotions were taken all in vain

he was the one who made her happy and silent,
her words were all calmly violent.

He was the one who cannot go away,
for her, his love will forever stay.

She wanted to give her soul and heart,
for they will never be apart.

She had a love for him in her eyes,
but he was the one who didn't realize.

Her tears were falling for that one and only,
her fake smile was telling that UNTOLD STORY.

Mahrukh Laeeq

A Writer

Since childhood, I always wanted to be a poetess or a writer. An expression through writing makes a better and a well understanding person, but deep down inside I always wanted to be someone's poem. As I grew up I realized lucky are those who are writers, poets or poetess, but luckiest are those who are someone's subject or a poem. Yes, they make you immortal in their writings, in their thoughts, because somehow people die but feelings never!

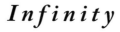

Infinity

Did you find your soul mate, a question brought by your fate?
Was your stomach filled with butterflies?
Or just you believed on all white lies?

Is there any space and time, where your hope lives and shines?
Will his feelings remain?
Or a love where your emotions can't be drained.

Did you ever look back at your past, took a
deep breath and have ever asked?
For what clustered memories brought you with,
And let you hold the emotional twig.

Did you think that a second will last, and found
your feelings like a broken glass?
If you found his love forever,
Didn't you freeze that imaginative endeavor?

Do you wonder or just you think?
Time flies in an eye blink.
Has it ever crossed your mind?
Memories are never defined….

Mahrukh Laeeq

Nostalgia

She accidentally starts looking at the sky, the evening is austere,
playing children make her dive into the heavy frost of past,
where friends pop out, bash into gossips and crack jokes.
Where mom's hand patting on head gives you a sigh of relief, where
Dad's Love make you feel blissful.
She steps into the misty place, where life is not a life, the
journey is not a journey rather a tedious route of past. An
abstract imagination highlighted with soulful relations.
Engraved in heart where a voice of someone makes her smile,
where a look of someone makes her drowned in the aromas
of the memories that take her to the trail of happiness.
The flashback of the listening shoulder takes her to the other world,
where few laughter's seems to be a treat for her heart. She speaks of
a memory where evening is full of joy, where she sees her siblings
holding her, laughing, cracking jokes about someone special.
Where her childhood reverts back, where her acts are
marked by different attributes, where people are marked
not by their names, but by their memories.
She tries to build a castle of her memories. Accidently, she stepped
into the real world where she smiles to hide her craggy emotions.
Where she lives to hide her broken heart, where she gets silent to
hide desolation of her heart, where she laughs to hide the vortex
of darkening grief, where she tries to sleep to hide her tears.
But those memories take her to the road of
happiness, that light in long darkness,
The light that guides her home.

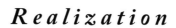

Realization

Today I am crying for all the odds
For myself, for an incomplete work
For my experience and principles,
For the bird that never gave me a message,
For that color that wasn't mine,
For that breeze that never entered my life.

Tomorrow I'll cry for every heart that I broke,
Every promise that I didn't mean,
That moment which never happened.

But someday someone will have my tears,
That day I'll not cry for myself but for someone else.

Mahrukh Laeeq

An Answer

Once he asked how much do you love me?
I was speechless at that time because words were escaping me
Now when he has gone, I found an answer to his question.
I write because he still exists in me,
my love made him immortal.

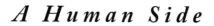

A Human Side

Everyone has a bleak side,
Nearest to skeleton they intend to hide.
Blur memories that they don't want to go,
Injured feelings that they can't afford to show.

Past that will blur never,
that second which lasted forever.
The memories where you try to outrun,
and suddenly the past comes undone.

Sunless skies and cloudy hearts,
where heartily feelings were ripped apart.
A tender look and soothing face,
taking you back to the happy place.

Yesterday turning to fuzzy past,
this moment and journey this too shall pass,
for they say life is an hour glass.
Since its GOOD BYES that I hate the most,
yet ships sailing away from coast.

Yes, we will be together once again,
remembering those moments and will laugh like insane.

Maybe it would be a misty morning and vivid past,
we shall recall our journey that was lost,
settling again in heavy frost.
Will again pile up our lifetime clicks,
till the time will play its frowsy trick.

Mahrukh Laeeq

The First Kiss

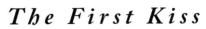

The silent evening marked with pain,
cloudy feelings and the pouring rain;

the moments he held my hands,
marking our memories on wet sand;

my worries, my tears, my breath was all taken,
our love, our feelings, were awaken.

Momentarily, he snatched me from all sorrows
and took me to the heavenly bliss.
I found myself in ecstasy, when he whispered and silently kissed.

An Art

God has made you an art, because you are a thought that
dances in my imagination, where no one can see you

Buried Deep

She says nothing is left between us, but still her
heart skips a beat when she thinks of him.

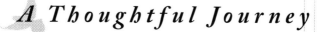

A Thoughtful Journey

You were the reason of my pain
like nothing was left sane,

But look, what I've saved for you
look at the castle of my dreams for you,

Only now can I find you
and recognize my blur vision
on your damaged decision.

Only now can I find you,
aimed at taking out my breath
that made you celebrated my timeless death.

Mahrukh Laeeq

The Girl with the Bunny Slippers

There were days when she wished she could step into her bunny slippers. Peep out of the window collect all the fairy dust that God sent to her. So, she could go in the fairy cart to the sky with angels and shoot firework with them, then to talk to God. So, He can dress her with hopes with shared smiles. Then she would slowly return to earth, step out of her bunny slippers and would get back to the bed, not necessarily in that order.

Wedding Ring

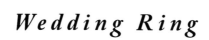

Her love was played,
like the guitar's strings;

On her lips silence sings,
in the cold rain he left,
by giving her the wedding ring.

Soul mate

I think it's perhaps when you have the bad habit of caring about everyone, even when no one notices your small gestures, and take you for granted when you love people too much, they don't even love you back. When you develop deepest affection for everyone and let them destroy you. This Fragile heart becomes your biggest weakness and you realize it's your fault. Yes, your fault. No one really understands you, but finding a soul who shares the same weakness as yours is perhaps, **a soul mate for me**!

Maturity

Maturity is when you are able to care about those relations, that hurt you the most. When you stop hurting people who once hurt you. It's simple, when you are able to fight with your conscious and sub-conscious, when you enter into the acceptance zone of life, when you know your acts won't harm others, when you realize the worth and value of emotion behind the situation rather than a situation and ***when you are able to confront your deepest fears.***

Once a silly girl

A silly girl, crying hard realized one day Sometimes it's not about who understands you, sometimes it's about who WANTS to understand you.

And Life's Dilemma

The more you trust the more you are betrayed, the more you love the more you are left alone, the more you smile, the more you are hurt, but sometimes few people are worth living for...

When She Misses You

She wakes up and thinks of you first,
she talks and talks about you just,
she sees in you her trust.
Now listen,
when she is hurt, she wishes to see you,
when she is lost, she prays to have you,
when her life gets dead, she searches an angel like you
she doesn't sleep,
because your absence makes her weep.
Her life gets dread and dew,
when she silently misses you.

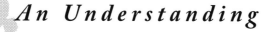

An Understanding

You are terrifying in your actions,
deep in your emotions,
a faultless defaulter,
unpredictable in life,
strange in reality,
interesting in your moods,
a child in an adult,
beautiful in your own way
not everyone knows how to hold on,
a beginning or an anticipation?
you are a moment in between.
You are a crux of my understanding...!

Mahrukh Laeeq

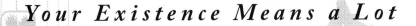

Your Existence Means a Lot

Do you want to know what makes you so worthwhile?
it's because when people got me,
I was fearless,
I was happy,
I was emotionally unused,
I believed in fairytale romance.
When you got me, I was bruised,
I was shattered, I was broken,
I was hurt.
I was afraid of life, I was afraid of love,
I was afraid of people and I was afraid to trust,
and yet you stayed to listen to me and
made me a whole again!

Because You are An Angel

I have known you for months,
in the darkest centuries of my life,
I have known you for hours in the brightest days of mine,
I have known you when my crumbling heart broke
into pieces and you made it a whole again,
I was so undeserving, but you listened.
I broke-- you repaired, I wept --you embraced,
I bled --you rectified, I shushed-- you smiled
Thank you for making me a whole again!

Mahrukh Laeeq

I never thought that I'd find comfort in his thoughts

Resistance

For they say time heals everything but time doesn't. It's just the way you lie to yourself just to make it resistible and that's how the life goes on....

Smile

Out of world's smiles, you have my favorite

A Broken Heart

When life gets dead, and the tears shed,
she silently cries, remembers the promises and often tries,
the memories make her weep,
she is unable to sleep and the love turns and prays, as the promise fades
the dawn has arisen, a life sad and blue
she closes her eyes and usually thinks of you,
now they're apart.
You'll be back, this is the only hope that lasts.
She dies every day,
how broken is her heart?

Mahrukh Laeeq

Agony

It's easy to move on when you are lost,
it's easy to fall in love,
it's easy to hide your emotions behind a big smile,
it's easy to feel every word of someone,
it's easy to own people who never bothered about you,
but it's anguishing to be stuck to the destiny, where you don't belong,
because that's the point where you unwantedly **agonize**.

A Random Diary Page

Going through life hardest moments, forgetting all the beautiful past, recollecting all your determination with your failures, rising and falling from your journey, weeping with hopelessness you accidentally find a page in your diary and that rotten flower which still has the same fragrance, it's fragrance not only bring those beautiful moments back, but it brings that beautiful person back in your life who was always there for you whenever you fell. That page not only brings the beautiful moments altogether, but that feel when someone held your hand looked into your eyes and said "everything will be fine", and that old diary page brings life to your lifeless journey. Sometimes just a small page can bring your whole beautiful journey back.

Miracles happen!

Insanity

I don't know what insanity is actually, but for me it's waiting for someone you love the most, waking up in the morning recalling that morning wish with a toast and coffee, recalling that evening where you both once walked on a tedious route with a camera in your hand and talking about your future plans, recalling that moment where someone gently made you feel special in spite of knowing he will never come back and you will never surrender.
It hurts, it hurts because it matters!

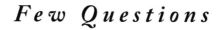

Few Questions

How did you find him asked the present?
"It was like finding pearl from the shores of sea, the
happiness from the perpetual silence present in me."
How did you love him, asked the prayer.
"He was the one on whom every breath was spent,
my life was spent, my soul was sacrificed but I never
expressed, brought with the flash of hope."
How it was to be loved? asked the joy.
"It was all amendment of my broken heart to see the
ray of light after the centuries of darkness."
How you felt when you were hurt? asked the grief.
"It was like laughing loud and loud and crying hard all at once"
How it was when you lost him? asked the luck.
After a long pause, I replied
"it was like every gasp of my breath happened all at once."

Mahrukh Laeeq

Comprehension

So, we finally decided to solve the mystery of our relationship
I trust you, he said,
are you going to tell me?
ready?
Yes ready, I replied.
you loved me that's it,
you cared for me for so many years, but this time you
badly broke my trust. Now, I don't trust myself for
trusting you. Let's close this chapter. That's it!
He looked into my eyes, and replied:
"You folded my lifetime sincerity in just a
chapter, you're my favorite book.
I won't be reading its last chapter ever, then
deeply sighed and said THATS IT!!"

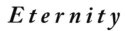

Eternity

Lucky are those who are poets and poetess but
luckiest are those who are their poems

Meaning

Life is not about having beautiful, rich and prosperous people around, sometimes it's just about a silent care and an understanding shoulder.

And That Last Moment

She was lying on her bed, folding her diary pages and these pages were not just pages rather the chapters of her life. Tears fell down her all prayers, those blood red eyes, those happy moments, the echoes of laughers recalling when someone held her hands, when hearts are broken, realizing worth of togetherness. Few moments if marked with compassion and realization turns into life time journey, that brought tears to her eyes but time is never constant its always chasing in a wicked game, suddenly the desires and hopes were all crumpled. Fate hurts she said to herself, then she silently marked her existence with happiness to move on, but somehow the promises, the trust would still remain in the lock closet of broken hearts. She then took a deep breath. After a while, she realized he was on the same chapter as she, but love and compatibility are not the same thing, she took a deep sigh and slept.

Words

"Words are most powerful, they can be medicine or a weapon, either they can heal a heart or can annihilate it."

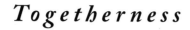

Togetherness

When she was with him, she lived only then.

No pain, no suffering, no worry, but only the

moment of togetherness.

Want

She sold out her heart to him
So, she can merge herself in his being
She kept her insanity in control,
For it was the only evidence of her incomparable love for him.

You

Life turns in a wonderful way,
as thoughts are scattered whenever I lay.

The time has changed,
my feelings for you are sensitive and strange.

I whisper softly,
my Love enhances for you quietly.

The promise that we keep,
glows in me till my life's asleep

I sacrificed my soul in a hue,
because NO one else can ever be like YOU.

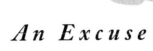

An Excuse

When you are with me nothing matters,
time and space both are shattered.

You become the clouds, the sky, the rain,
and my.... eternal gain.

You are the beautiful rose that blossoms,
in the leaves that are crumpled, in the gardens of autumn.

You are the eternity present in me,
for the love that brings a spirit of the sea.

I wish I can freeze our moments in evening hues,
before the remorseless time, be yours excuse...!!!

On Your Birthday

She took a pen to write on you,
her words are lost when she thinks of you.
She somehow manages to rise and gets through,
but she falls again when she thinks of you.
She looks up to sky if you rest there,
the laughers, the moments, the smile you shared.
Then she climbed the ladder to the sky,
walked on the silver lining, her feelings very high.
Built you a Lego house of neon lights,
because she wanted to see you at heavenly heights.
She planted the flowers of hope there,
to pleasantly surprise you and to care.
She shot fireworks with angels to celebrate your day,
it crackled on earthy people and the laughter that stayed.
They saw a visible lantern light that adheres,
she then found you laughing on moonlight chair.
She closed her eyes to feel your presence,
the commitment, the hope the word that happened.
She opened her eyes to look around,
a glittering shadow and a light that surrounds.
She walked in the Lego house crossed all sad and blues,
no voice, no hope but deepest clues.
She somehow managed to write on you,
your words, your existence how long they will stay,
but her words and feelings were all at bay.
She lived once and died again,
her spirit tasted a holy stay,
it was all ON YOUR BIRTHDAY

Mahrukh Laeeq

Commitment

That night has gone,
when you came to me on thorns.

And made me a promise to stay forever,
won't hurt and would never make my trust shatter.

On every rising dawn,
you gave me a hope and our love was reborn.

In every evening shine,
you gave me the purity of your time,

and....
Made me feel you are mine.

A new day has begun
I search for you to make our lives heaven.

Your memories are now heaped,
I miss you and I silently weep.

Be with me forever in this life track,
I miss you a lot,
PLEASE COME BACK!

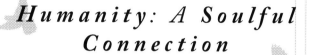

Humanity: A Soulful Connection

There are no enclosures for us,
for we are free birds on the sky of earth.

Our souls are wings in this world,
flying out to meet the perpetuity.

How can we all be separated from each other?
For we are all interconnected,
holding our heartbeats in each other's hearts.

Why should we worry where will we go?
For our destinations are all same;

we will remain with each other,
in hearts ---being heartbeats.

Peace

She wanted to weep as much as she could,
when he sat opposite to her, she couldn't cry as
she knew he was lost in her melancholy.
He was as broken and as sad as she was,
she knew if she cried he would be broken too,
Indeed, it was a huge effort they managed to sit
without even saying a word to each other,
by hiding their bursting emotions.
Their words were not words, but bruised
feeling which were not said but felt,
with every second that passed by, was giving
vivid interpretation of silence,
they came from the dale of peace.

Remorseless Fate

Come and be with me my beloved
let's go to the paradise
for that way is only known to you,
let us see the sunshine above
let us belong to the glittering stars
let the sky be our mirror;

come and be with me my beloved
let us enjoy the dust of past,
let us enjoy the raindrop of our eyes
which shine like a pearl in our destiny,
let us feel the beauty of our scars
for they show our rigorous struggle;

Come and be with me my beloved
let us see the wrinkles in our life,
for they are the souvenirs to us
let us feel the beauty of melancholy,
for it tells us the worth of happiness
let us dissolve in the tedious question mark;

Until the fate makes the destiny DARK!

Mahrukh Laeeq

Existence

She was lost in his thoughts,
until she found an easy way out.
She made him her heartbeat, and merged her existence into his.
Now he was never distant, she crossed the journey
of time and space in just a moment.
For he became her existence!

Jugular vein

Leave this game
Just fill your heart with peace
and let the rest go away.
Leave all these games and be kind to yourself.
Be true to your core where love stays.
Go after your instinct like a resonance of this universe,
see your beloved's face in the blood running in your veins.
Drink holy water in the strange hostelry of love.
You don't have to see him daily,
Just look in the mirror and see his face,
go follow your heart for he, is your jugular vein!

Until the Grave

First, there were the diaries
painted blues,
with hearts in miseries
and that morning dew.
The feelings in sparkling ink,
commitment that blinked.
The scent of words in each phrase,
the cards with all the paints,
the dried rose in a diary.
Each page was filled with the memory,
in letters' some dried up petals,
betrayed love that nettles
inside a memory clutch.
The last letter in her hand,
a memory where she still stands,
and his scent that was divine,
she will carry him for lifetime
in her writings, he shines.
And would forever in her inks and pens,
in each memory orchid, of every trend,
until her bones and mud are being blend

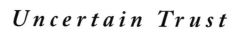

Uncertain Trust

Is this trust?
If she must possess:
The eyes beholding the universe
and a soul of a radiant lake
for memories to take the dive,
anticipating a harvest of gems
where, dreams do not reside.
"Tell me is this trust?"
If it's long soft locks that must
ensure frame-up in
a cabalistic snare
and not what's
in a life to offer.
While,
the confined thoughts enchant the cynics,
who otherwise won't be attracted
to surplus a second
"Tell me, is this trust?"

when the black and whites are only visible
and greys are ignored,
making the tedious maps of memories
greys and lines or
demonic designs;
pulling all long calculations of emotions
will the over looker be subjective?
And see the reality?
Tell me what is this then?
"If not, the Uncertain trust!!"

I Wait, I Do Not Wait

I wait for you to love me,
I do not wait for you to love me.
I wait to be in your thoughts,
I do not wait to be in your thoughts.
I think of you every night,
I do not think of you every night.
I cry hard for loving you,
I do not cry hard for loving.
I wait that I'll be in your thoughts,
I do not wait that I will be in your thoughts.
For I am you,
my existence is yours and your existence is mine.
Strange melancholy your love has brought to me,
strange love you have brought to me,

for I will always wait for you...

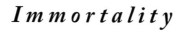

Immortality

I will celebrate every bruise of mine,
for it is a gift, by you in a boundless time.

I will live by thinking of you,
So, you stay with me in all my blues.

I will always write in greys,
So, you remain immortal and forever stay.

Intimacy

Like the composition of music and the emotions in poetry, nothing
was closer to her than the silent understanding in their relation.

A Spirit Of The Sea

I want to be the beautiful sky, that makes you wonder;
I want be the fiery emotion, that makes you miss me;
I want be an intense sponge, that consumes your sorrows;
I want be the blaze, that burns your agony;
I want to be your jugular vein, so I can be closer than you.
Pick whoever as you like to...
But be a spirit of the sea.

Mahrukh Laeeq

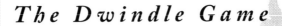

The Dwindle Game

It wasn't with the time,
the bruise unhealed;
when she wept on her knees
that lasted in her mind.

It wasn't with the swords,
when she was killed;
but with the hesitation in words
and the love was instilled.

While, she was caged in pain,
for him, her love was a game,
but her heart had only his name
which he won, over and over again.

Offender

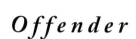

O perpetual offender,
Pluck the flower,
and breathe life into death!
I know everything through you:
poetry, paintings, love, and pain!

O perpetual offender,
I am wrapped in time-lapse,
pain and a thousand ambiguities!
Peel layer after layer of my soul,
here lies the well of sorrows buried deep down!

O perpetual offender,
Serve me insanity, death and love under the illusionary peaceful sky.

Mahrukh Laeeq

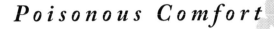

Poisonous Comfort

It is astonishing....
How he loved her in happiness and left her in cold to mortify!
It is astonishing...
How did he septic the hallucination of affection when he served it to her!
She thickly asked her soul:
Why should she still remain merged in his existence?
Why shouldn't she separate herself and live with herself...
After a long aching pause,

she realized:
"She cannot abandon herself from him for he
became her blood running in her veins,
he took her away with him"

Promise

He promised to love her forever, but then she
realized promises are meant to be broken!!!

A Poet

Who is a poet? A person who seeks happiness
and fulfillment of everyone's emotions.
Poet is not just subjective. A person who unintentionally starts
feeling everyone's pain, absorbing them just like a sponge. A person
who holds sadness and melancholy deep down his soul, but is able
to make everyone happy. Whose lips are formed to be silent, but
fingers are meant to be spoken. This person is like a sensitive rhythm,
that people want to hear again and again. These rhythmic flows
are just not some ordinary beats, but a sound of his sorrows that
would be a delightful pain for him and blissful for others to hear.

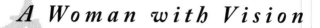

A Woman with Vision

A woman with the reminiscent light,
who burns herself for others, to shine.

Her sorrows are as dark as night,
but she is abstract with intensified sight.

She burns herself to ashes,
to masked her agony bright.

The tears that fall every day,
on the pages of her diary, before she writes.

Suffering

The moment in life when you start thinking you are strong enough, so strong that you can bear all pain alone. The moments that make you silent, the moment that whispers to you softly, YOU ARE BRAVE ENOUGH, you become so strong and so quiet that you forget that YOU ARE SUFFERING.

Winters Love

Start of winters
heart in bloom,

The silent whispers
in a decipher room,

his words were felt a little more
while she was thinking on a sea shore,

when December came with all its whites
her heart dropped in a dusky light,

he brought smiles on her face
till good bye was said, with a broken trace...!

A Lost Girl

In the glow of her eternal truth
when she had to learn about her youth,

in tears-soaked heart
she saw no hope, her smiles were all dark,

she should have gone by then
when her patience was tested till the end,

she was lost in the wrong hands
her emotions were his weapons for a timeless span,

As she trusted, she realized:

In the time of her swiftly youth,
she diffused her happiness in an ageless ruth.

The Thread

When you had me?
I was happy and free.
You wanted a person without scars,
who could take you in a boundless time.

Wasn't that I?
Who gave you what you wished for,
a moment that danced upon a broken line,

then someone else you met,
who offered you new colors instead,
and you picked her for a lifetime thread!

Eternal Pain

What have you desired for, deep down your heart?
When your hope does rise,
in the lifeless moments of past.

What do you ask for, when you see the stars?
Emotions as your weapon
or bruised feelings that will happen?

What do you look for, when you see the mirror?
a lost you,
or a broken swear?

You will get what you aim,
but live in the moments that are insane,
before time brings you,
its eternal pain!

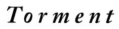

Torment

Most of the time it's not the bruises that hurt on the body,
It's the wounds in your feelings and scars on your life!

W h y

I faced a void within my soul,
it was vast--- like a vacuum;
it could bring down the skies,
and would never feel the victory.

I felt the hollow love
on the day, you came;
but you said me GOOD BYE,
and left me to cry.

The pain that you never faced
made my love all replaced;
and left me to die,
my heart would always wonder, *Why?*

Promises Hurt

Do you remember,
what you said to me?
That you would love me
until our souls set free.

Did you remember the promises you made?
And in reality, your love was strayed.

You told me, I was your strength and I was your weakness,
then why you left me in painful bleakness?

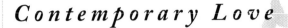

Contemporary Love

In the moments, all contemporary
the emotions are taken temporary;

for the people who leave their love and move on,
the worth of togetherness that's bygone;

the flower, the word, the promise,
the coldness that made it all vanish;

the precious moments never come back,
let's hold the love till lasting grief hijacks.

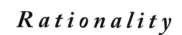

Rationality

Who finds rationality in love?
for love is born to be irrational.
Separating the logics and calculations and not
letting them interfere in warm emotions.
When calculations are added in love and emotions
are measured then time becomes remorseless.
For love is born free with the wings without cage of rationality, to be
nurtured because love is not a gain, it's not supposed to be measured.
It is supposed to be felt deep down the flesh,
bones or perhaps deeper.... SOUL!

Mahrukh Laeeq

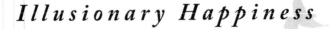

Illusionary Happiness

Let's make the best out of our lives
and risk not to dream more.
Not a single step we shall skip,
for the ones who made us ripped;

let's love people with the scars,
for they know life is an hour glass.
Do not dreams of broken emotions,
for today we'll speak, words unspoken.

Let's not dream for the blessings in disguise
or set our wishes by looking up to the sky;
at least once in a while we deserve to live,
let's dive in illusions, 'fore our souls are lift.

L o v e

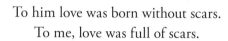

To him love was born without scars.
To me, love was full of scars.

I love you, I would say.
Love is not meant for the broken hearts, it has
a long magnitude, he would reply.

I couldn't jumble up the worlds to tell him the intensity of my emotions.
But he wanted love, as fresh as a flower ready to be
plucked that was the center of attraction for the people
around, a flower untouched, unseen and unheard.

For me flowers were known for their fragrance,
for their captivation, and to be fostered.

For him they were meant to be plucked.
For me they were meant to be nurtured.

But I loved him regardless of time and different emotions.
I wish I could tell him,
for me love means to stay forever, not as temporary as the plucked flower.
Is there any magnitude that lasts forever?

I wish I could have told him!

Mahrukh Laeeq

Parts Of Me

My writings are my identity, of my maverick soul,
the words that I am too afraid to say.
My writings are the pieces of my concealed feelings,
that are hidden under my flesh to stay.

My writings are my cognition with the highest frequencies,
that never matched the ruthless lies of fantasies'.

My writings are the unfinished rain dance,
and the time that once brought a mischance.

My writings are buried words that wouldn't drown or flee,
for they will always be the parts of me...!

A Special Note to My Husband

I would like to especially thank my husband in completion of this book. I think back to the first time, I laid my eyes on him and I knew right then that I had found someone incredible, loving and supportive. Ever since that very moment, all I have ever wanted was to be with him with all my heart and devotion. He has always encouraged me and motivated me to pursue my dreams. No matter what goes on in my life, I look forward to every moment of every day with him. Without him, my dreams would have been impossible to pursue. His support, love and encouragement mean the world to me. Without him, I would have never thought about publishing any of my writings.

Thank you, My Husband, for completely changing
my life in the best way possible!

Printed in the United States
By Bookmasters